**DO NOT REMOVE
CARDS FROM POCKET**

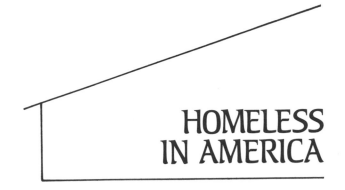

HOMELESS
IN AMERICA

HOMELESS IN AMERICA

BY ANNA KOSOF

FRANKLIN WATTS 1988
NEW YORK LONDON TORONTO SYDNEY

Photographs courtesy of:
United Nations: pp. 16, 20, 50;
UPI/Bettmann Newsphotos: pp. 19, 32, 36, 60, 94;
Bettye Lane: pp. 23, 25, 26, 42, 43, 46,
49, 57, 64, 69, 79, 81, 84, 92;
AP/Wide World Photos: p. 98.

Library of Congress Cataloging-in-Publication Data
Kosof, Anna.
Homeless in America / by Anna Kosof.
p. cm.
Bibliography: p.
Includes index.
Summary: Discusses the problem of homelessness in the United
States, the work of shelters, and the particular problems of
homeless children.
ISBN 0-531-10519-9
1. Homelessness—United States—Juvenile literature. 2. Homeless
persons—United States—Case studies—Juvenile literature.
[1. Homelessness. 2. Homeless persons.] I. Title.
HV4505.K67 1988
362.5'0973—dc19   87-26230 CIP AC

Copyright © 1988 by Anna Kosof
All rights reserved
Printed in the United States of America
6 5

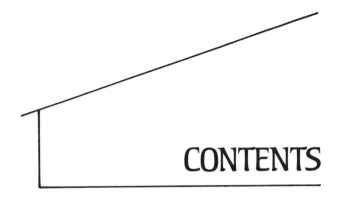

CONTENTS

This book is dedicated to the homeless, who gave me a new understanding of suffering, and survival. To Del, for his invaluable help and wisdom.

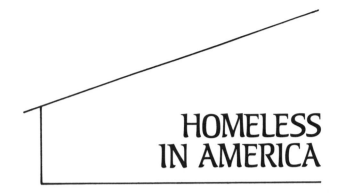

HOMELESS
IN AMERICA

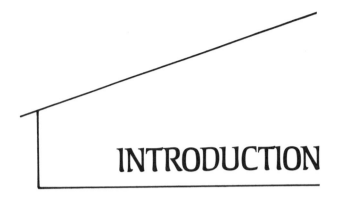

INTRODUCTION

"I never imagined that I'd be homeless." Although I heard this statement made over and over again, the facts behind it remain astonishing. More and more people are homeless in America, and in some places their numbers rival those of the Great Depression.

In 1984 the Reagan administration estimated the country's unhoused population at only 300,000,[1] a figure that has since been described as ridiculously low. Advocates for the Homeless, a national organization, estimate this population to be between two and three million.[2] No one really knows. What we *do* know about the homeless is that the number of people seeking shelter has increased dramatically. In 1983, 700 homeless families in New York City stayed in shelters; in 1987 there were more than 4,600. In January 1987, as temperatures dropped into the teens, a record number of 10,444 additional adults were given shelter at the city's twenty-one sites for single people, creating major overcrowding. While no one was turned away, at one facility more than 1,200 slept in a space normally allocated for 900.[3]

Eighty percent of the shelters in Chicago reported an increase in the demand for beds in 1985. Over sixteen thousand people were turned away because the shelters were full.

What do we know about today's homeless? We know the frightening fact that their numbers are growing faster than the surveys can count. We know, too, that they are not the same people as the bums and alcoholics of a bygone era, the old men on skid row who stood on street corners and slept in flophouses and doorways.

Since 1980, the country's homeless population has doubled every year. The age of the homeless has become lower, and the number of homeless children and homeless families has increased. Until recently, the homeless were stereotyped as people unworthy of help in obtaining food or shelter, as if they had created their own predicament. Some have suggested that the homeless prefer to live on the streets, including President Reagan, who said in 1984, ". . . one problem that we've had even in the best of times, and that is the people who are sleeping on the grates, the homeless are homeless, you might say, by choice." It is easier and more comfortable to assume that they are on the streets because they prefer to be there than to admit that many of them had no choice, either because the shelters were dangerous or because there simply were no vacancies.

According to a study done by the University of California at Los Angeles, 64 percent of the homeless in Los Angeles have been on the streets less than a year, 25 percent have finished high school, and 7.1 percent hold a bachelor's degree. Nationally, the average age of the homeless is thirty-four, a new low; 21 percent are family units comprising mostly single women and their children; in some areas, as many as one-third are Vietnam veterans.[4]

The results of a survey conducted in 1984 by the New York City Human Resources Administration concurred with those statistics. The survey found that the average age of those in shelters was thirty-five and that 49 percent of the single men had a high school education compared with 57 percent of the women. According to the same study, 25 percent were found to be "chronically mentally ill," yet over 80 percent of the men and 70 percent of the women received no form of public assistance.[5]

"Homelessness is a massive epidemic, so overwhelming that the problem must be treated as a national emergency,"[6] a congressional committee report declared recently.

What happened? What changed? The United States is the country that so proudly sent food to the starving people of Africa, the war-ravaged populations of Europe. We are accustomed to aiding the poor in other lands. And we all recall the hungry children with torn clothing, living on the streets, portrayed in novels by Charles Dickens and John Steinbeck. But now we are talking about millions of homeless in America who also live on the streets and in shelters and overcrowded "welfare" hotels—people who sleep in doorways, in bus stations, on subways, and in churches.

As Martin Begun of the N.Y.U. Medical Center puts it, "Soon the street dwellers will become part of the scenery, much in the way that the poor and starving in Calcutta are no longer seen as human beings but as part of the local color. . . . In our success-oriented society, we do not like failures and we think of incurable diseases and dependent people who will need constant care as failures."[7]

This book is the story of the homeless. It is their story, one that tells who they are, how they became homeless, and what their lives are like as people living without fulfillment of the most basic human needs. It is not a pretty story. It is a story filled with pain and disappointment—a story of inhumanity but also a story of compassion and caring.

We will meet many of the homeless. Their stories are as fascinating as those of the people behind any stories, and they are surprisingly all different. Some of the homeless are mentally disabled; some are drug addicts; some are poor; some lost their homes through fire, flood, or tornado; others were evicted; others endured long hospital stays; still others were just plain unlucky and had no financial resources to fall back on when disaster struck. They all have one thing in common, however—they are all homeless.

While some may argue that the homeless are far removed from us, the fact remains that everyone in the United States is now aware of poverty, hunger, and homelessness. We have seen the homeless in Arizona, in Iowa, and in Missouri. They are a constant presence in the parks of Santa Monica, California, a half mile from million-dollar homes. They are on nightly television programs, along with news reporters pretending to live the lives of the homeless, attempting to understand the humiliating experience of being hungry, cold, and homeless, if only for one night. The reporters, however, know that the very next day they will be home in their warm beds in their own homes. The homeless are not pretending for just one night or just a few. These are their lives. They live them every day, some for many years.

This is also a story about the will to live—to survive in subzero weather, to find shelter nightly, to be a scavenger, to find food daily in garbage cans outside restaurants, to collect discarded cans and bottles to return in exchange for a meager sum of money.

In New York City, where more than 30,000 are homeless, it is estimated that one person dies every day from the effects of living on the streets. It is surprising that only one person a day dies. It seems a miracle that the others survive, living through the most degrading experiences. Most of them have been mugged and robbed; some have been raped or seen others killed.

Some of the homeless have survived as such for years. They seem to have the ability and the desire to live against all the odds. One can only respect their determination. They are enduring what most people cannot even imagine —the profoundly frightening experience of being homeless.

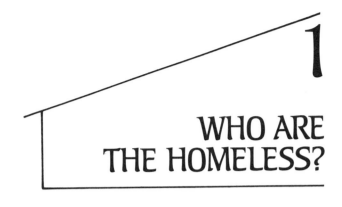

WHO ARE
THE HOMELESS?

"Homeless!" To most of us the true meaning of that word is inconceivable. We have no idea what it's really like to be homeless. Think about all the things that we take for granted. It would seem reasonable to assume that in the most affluent country in the world—where many people own homes and boats and summer houses worth more than most people in other countries earn in their entire lifetimes, where more people buy Rolls-Royces than in any other country in the world—everyone has food and shelter. And yet, Santa Monica, a section of Los Angeles where property values are among the highest in the world, with homes worth over a million dollars, has one of the largest homeless populations in this country. In the United States, the number of people who have no permanent homes—no place to live, no place to eat, no place called "home"—is estimated in the millions.

The homeless have no address, and because they don't stay in one place, it is very hard to count them. Some live on the streets, some in shelters, some in trailer trucks on campsites, while still others are staying temporarily with friends or relatives, often the first step to homelessness.

What does it really feel like to be without a home?

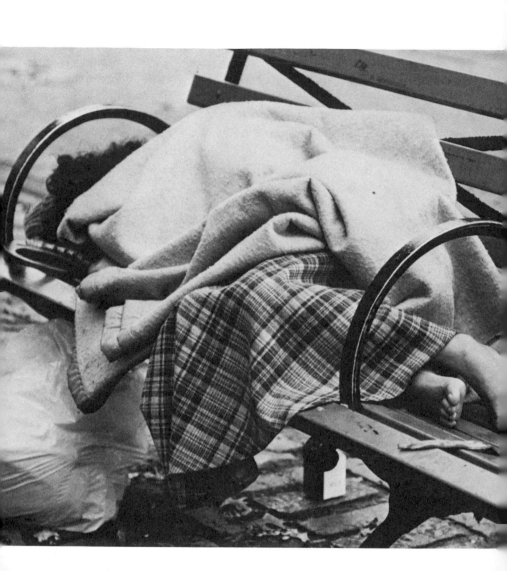

*The average age of the homeless is
thirty-four. Here, a homeless woman
sleeps on a park bench.*

No one who is fortunate enough to have a home can truly imagine what it is like to be without one. It is the most precious thing that we can have, yet we assume that we all have a place to call our own, a place we can lock and where we keep our material possessions and special belongings, a place to go home to. Home is a place we take for granted, while hundreds of thousands of people across the country go to sleep on the sidewalks, in public rest rooms, in bus depots, in makeshift homes on highways, in church basements temporarily turned into as shelters, and in public shelters that house over a thousand people, offering nothing more than a sea of beds placed next to each other. The homeless have no permanent beds, few clothes, and no kitchens in which to prepare their food. The children have few toys. Most of all, they have no place to call their own, no place to put their few belongings.

From the very beginning of time, people have waged war for food and shelter. In the most primitive societies, they have struggled to meet these most basic human needs. It is astonishing that in the twentieth century, we are still struggling to fill these needs. In early primitive societies, people banded together to search for food and shelter, traveling from place to place, defending themselves against dangers. Today the homeless travel alone or with only small children and without the protection of a group.

While most people will never know the experience of scavenging for food or searching for a place to sleep every night, perhaps by reading the stories of the homeless, people will be better able to understand their plight—how they became homeless, how they lost most of their material possessions, and how they survived.

For many of the homeless, their misfortune was caused by external forces. Although many poor people lost their homes in fires or other disasters, more have become homeless because over one million—almost half the country's total—SRO (single-room occupancy) units were lost in the 1970s.[8] They had housed a great number of elderly and poor people, as well as those released from mental institutions. In New York City alone, 100,000 SROs were demolished to make way for urban renewal, upgrading of neighborhoods, and the construction of condominiums and luxury apartments. SROs had been affordable for low-wage earners, retired people on fixed incomes, and welfare recipients who were allotted small amounts for rent. As SROs were demolished or converted to house upper-income people, the poor people living in these units were frequently put out on the streets without notice. Often they had no place to go. Their welfare checks could not pay for similar housing because similar housing was not available. Without resources, without money to pay high rent, they found themselves on the streets. Some of them had limited educations and didn't know they were entitled to help from government agencies, or they simply didn't know how to deal with the bureaucratic red tape that government assistance involves.

Another large group that became homeless—as a result of government policies—is composed of former mental patients. During the 1960s a new attitude developed in the United States about the mentally ill. The plight of chronically mentally ill Americans today is a direct result of the nation's twenty-year experimentation with "deinstitutionalization," the release from state-run asylums and return to their home communities of chronic mental patients. This was made possible by major breakthroughs in the development of new drugs for the treatment of schizophrenia and

The face of the homeless is one of desperation and defeat. This man is one of thousands in Los Angeles who received a hot turkey dinner provided by a local church at Thanksgiving 1986.

other mental illnesses. It was thought that instead of housing the mentally ill in large, inhumane state institutions at an astronomical cost, it would be better to return them to their communities, where they could lead more independent lives. As long as they took their medication regularly, the authorities believed, these people could function outside institutions.

In 1963, President John F. Kennedy signed the Community Mental Health Centers Act to create a network of aftercare centers to help these people reenter society. The plan was to build more than two thousand small housing units in communities where the mentally ill could live with some supervision. However, most of these community residences were never built; only about seven hundred were actually completed. Thus, many of the people who lived in state institutions were discharged to fend for themselves. Some moved into SRO hotels and rooming houses, which were their only affordable options. Others moved to the streets and the shelters. All these people had emotional or mental disabilities and were in need of care and medical attention. Yet they were placed in situations that provided no care, no medical attention, and no security.

The populations of state and county facilities dropped by nearly 450,000 between 1955 and 1984. It is true that the majority of these "liberated" mental patients, 65 percent, have adapted to life on the outside. But for the rest, thousands of former inmates, deinstitutionalization turned out to be a hoax. As one psychiatrist, Dr. Stephen Rachlin, commented, "Liberty to be psychotic is not 'freedom' in

A large portion of the homeless are former mental patients, released from institutions and returned to home communities that have no aftercare centers for their supervision.

any responsible sense of the word."[9] Often released with medication they were expected to take daily in order to function, frequently they didn't know where their medication was or simply forgot to take it. It seems unthinkable that people most in need of help would be put in situations that totally healthy individuals with all their mental faculties intact would find challenging. Many of these people were reluctant to go into shelters. Left on the streets or in bus depots, they have had the greatest difficulty fending for themselves. But because they are among the most brutalized in city shelters, many of them choose to stay on the streets. Some of them are dangerous to themselves and to society.

Clearly, the plan to humanize the treatment of mental patients backfired sharply, creating a significant portion of the homeless. It is estimated that in some areas of the country, as many as 30 to 40 percent of the hard-core homeless—the people on the streets for the longest periods of time—are those former mental patients, the by-product of a poorly executed government policy.

Another major contributor to the homeless problem is the lack of low-income housing. Since the passage of the Federal Housing Act of 1939, approximately 87 percent of all money to build low-income housing has come from the federal government. This legislation grew out of the understanding that the private construction industry would build the most profitable housing instead of low-income housing, even though the latter was badly needed. But the Reagan administration has virtually put a stop to the financing of low-income housing, creating in some places waiting lists of 15,000 people and delays of up to twenty-five years to get into 6,000 low-income units. At the same time, since 1983 the federal budget has earmarked only $70 million a

Among the homeless are Vietnam veterans.

year for direct aid to the homeless, about one-third of what New York City spent in 1984 alone.

We can begin to see a picture developing. Two sets of homeless people were created by government policies that directly affected people's lives and their shelter. While state mental institutions were brutal places that did not provide much care or treatment, the lack of community facilities resulted in many of the mentally ill living on the streets. Many of them are entitled to Social Security and welfare benefits, but they don't know they are entitled to payments or don't know how to obtain them. Moreover, social service departments will not issue benefit checks without an address for the recipient. Since those who live on the streets have no address, they cannot get checks and cannot afford a place to live. A social worker told the story of explaining this "crazy" policy to someone who just came out of a mental institution. After the patient listened to this explanation a few times, she stormed out of the social worker's office, yelling, "And you think that *I'm* the one who's crazy? *You're* the ones who are crazy!" She continued to mutter to herself, "I can't get no check because I ain't got no address, and I can't get no place to live because I ain't got no money. They're really crazy in there. I'm never going back there."

According to the *New York Times*, it is estimated that in New York City the cost of housing for a family of four in a barrackslike shelter in the Bronx has risen to $70,000 a year. "It is unconscionable to pay that kind of money and keep families in these conditions," State Commissioner of Social Services Cesar Perales declared.[10] Yet the city spends millions of dollars to house people in barracks, in large gymnasiums that are nothing more than rows of cots, in neighborhoods where it isn't safe for children to play outside. Still, these homeless people aren't eligible to receive a welfare check for $247 a month, the amount allotted for rent in New York City, because they have no address.

Children constitute the most frightening group of homeless. The number of teenage single mothers is rising

-24

A homeless teenager with her baby on the streets of New York City

*Two homeless women become friends.
Henrietta, left, was burned out of her
Harlem apartment. As a result of being
attacked by a man wielding a metal rod,
she may lose her right eye. Doris, right,
a battered wife, was thrown out of her
home by her husband, who threatened
her with more violence if she returned.*

at an epidemic rate, and it is estimated that in some parts of the country 20 percent of the homeless are children of single parents. Often the parents are unable to afford the rents that many neighborhoods require. Again, they begin by living with family or friends, but after a short period of time, they find that they have to get out and find another place to stay. Often they simply cannot find a place to live because they cannot afford the rent.

Some, living in run-down tenements or other marginal places, lose their homes because of fire. Many buildings are destroyed by arson, often instigated by the landlords in order to evict the tenants and renovate the buildings for higher rents.

New York City's Human Resources Administration estimates that homelessness in the city rose 500 percent between 1980 and 1987. Obviously, a 500 percent increase means that this problem is created in part by governmental and societal policies, not merely by a handful of people who are crazy or addicted to drugs or alcohol.

People without boots cannot pull themselves up by their bootstraps. They cannot find homes if there are none to be found. Whether it comes from the federal government or the state, they need help, more than any private effort can provide. Until they get it, they have no place to turn but to the cold, mean streets.

HOMELESS IN
THE HEARTLAND

We might think that all homeless people live in urban centers, in big cities. We might think of New York City or Los Angeles or Chicago, but we don't think of Arizona and Iowa. But the homeless live there, too. They are everywhere. Whether the state is Iowa, Arizona, or New York, some of the ingredients for becoming homeless are the same. While Iowa and Arizona are predominantly white (both states' populations are more than 90 percent white) and New York's poor and homeless population is predominantly black and Hispanic, in this chapter we focus on those areas usually not associated with poverty and homelessness.

Perhaps what makes Arizona unique is that no other state has erected more obstacles for the homeless. Despite rapid increases in the number of homeless people in both large and small cities throughout Arizona, authorities have placed barrier after barrier in the way of obtaining relief.

In order to be considered eligible for Arizona's Emergency Assistance (EA) Program, the state declared that a homeless family must have a legally dependent child or be deemed eligible for General Assistance. However, to be deemed eligible, a homeless individual must have a written statement, signed by a doctor or psychiatrist, certifying un-

-29

employability because of medical reasons. In addition, homeless families or individuals are ineligible to receive EA during a month in which they receive out-of-state entitlements. The EA level is set at $100 per month for the head of the household, with $25 given for each additional family member. Therefore, not only are there obstacles to receiving assistance, but the level of assistance would not support a family adequately.

That the people of Arizona are increasingly experiencing housing problems is reflected in the number of evictions and foreclosures taking place there. Legal Services of Phoenix—an organization that gives legal aid to the poor, including advice regarding evictions—handled 735 such cases in 1982, and by 1983 that figure rose to 976, a 33 percent increase. The rate of increase has risen dramatically each year since then.

Like many other states, Arizona lacks adequate services for the mentally ill. Of the estimated 300 state-funded community residence beds in Arizona, 216 are located in Phoenix, another 45 in Tucson, and another 18 in Yuma. Arizona's chronic mentally ill population has been estimated at some 8,000. Many of these individuals have no place to turn to but the streets.

Arizona was chosen as one focal point of this book because this state provides one of the most vivid pictures of how so many authorities treat the homeless. Arizona's inhumanity in ridding the Phoenix downtown area of homeless individuals has been especially blatant.

In 1984, in Phoenix, Arizona, there were 3,300 homeless men, women, and children, a figure representing a doubling since 1979 of people living without a permanent home in that city.[11] Since 1984 the figure has increased rapidly.

Like Phoenix, Tucson has also experienced a doubling of the number of individuals who became homeless in recent years. By 1984 there were nearly 2,000 homeless in Tucson.[12] Since that time the figure has steadily increased.

Tucson's Mayor Lewis Murphy publicly declared, "The last thing we want to do is provide amenities to homeless individuals." Because of this official attitude toward the homeless, the city had only two soup kitchens in the mid-1980s. The operators of these facilities fought an uphill battle with city agencies and citizens' groups to remain open.

As if that were not painful enough, the city council appointed a task force charged with developing a proposal for a correctional facility that could be used to jail those homeless arrested for trespassing, panhandling, and other minor crimes. Clearly, the state's attitude was to blame the victims and treat the homeless as criminals.

Depending on the climate and the geographic area, the homeless use different public places as shelter. While in New York City, Grand Central Station is a common place to keep warm, in Portland, Oregon, they built a shantytown under a bridge, with tents and outdoor cooking facilities. In Prescott, Arizona, on the border of a national forest in the northern part of the state, homeless people live in the forest in the summer.

In 1980, early in the homeless explosion, the Phoenix City Council formed an ad hoc committee to find a solution to the homeless problem. Ironically, the committee found that "it was the providers of emergency services who were attracting the homeless poor to the area." They also noted, "Missions and social services catering to the transient and public inebriate population should be encouraged to relocate on a voluntary basis and in a dispersed pattern, to areas outside central Phoenix."[13] Furthermore, they initiated strict laws prohibiting sleeping in public parks at night. In 1981 the City Council passed an ordinance making it a misdemeanor to lie down or sit on curbs, in alleys, or on streets; to urinate in public places; or to walk on private property where No Trespassing signs were posted. To make matters worse, the city condemned the buildings used by emergency shelter providers to make way for the new Civic Center. The following year, because of highway construction in the

This woman is one of some two hundred homeless people living on the banks of the Salt River near downtown Phoenix, Arizona.

area, they forced the Salvation Army to shut down its emergency shelter and its soup kitchen. Along with the loss of emergency shelters, twenty-two SRO hotels in the downtown area were closed, displacing over 1,000 people. By 1983, two studies of homeless people had been conducted by the Phoenix South Community Mental Health Center, in conjunction with the Salvation Army and the Saint Vincent de Paul Society.[14] These studies contradicted the popular myths that seem to surround the problem of homelessness. Contrary to the ad hoc committee's conclusions, which implied that homeless people wanted to be on the streets and that they purposely went to Arizona to be homeless, the studies found that 96 percent did not live on the streets by choice. Seventy-five percent of the homeless gave the search for employment as their reason for coming to Arizona. Only 22 percent were found to be alcoholics, and 25 percent were transients—people who were temporarily stranded in Arizona.

According to the Phoenix Consortium for the Homeless, who conducted a survey of all the SRO hotels and emergency shelters in the city, there were no vacancies. On one night during the period of the survey, the consortium found that because there were no vacancies, fifty people slept on the ground in Library Park, while dozens of others slept in cars.[15]

By 1983, the problem was so acute that—in the absence of emergency shelters, which had been closed by the local government—Tent City was established. Over 600 people were living in Tent City, which encompassed two parking lots. When the population of Tent City reached its peak, the Saint Vincent de Paul Society, with help from the Phoenix Consortium for the Homeless, rented a 220-person-capacity warehouse to be used for emergency shelter. At the same time, the Salvation Army agreed to establish an overflow facility in an old state-owned warehouse. Shortly after these shelters opened, the Phoenix establishment renewed its attack on the homeless. This time, the attack came from the business community, which established a Downtown Crime Task Force. The head of the task force put it very clearly: "The time is long overdue for running the bums out of downtown Phoenix and out of Phoenix altogether."[16] They encouraged people to report anyone panhandling, trespassing, littering, sleeping on public property, or lying on park benches. They perpetuated the myth that the homeless are petty criminals or bums who choose not to work, even though the studies conducted by the Phoenix Consortium for the Homeless proved otherwise. According to the studies, only 5 percent of homeless people could be classified as involved in criminal activities.

The picture in Arizona was grim. Like many others, government leaders refused to recognize the problem of homelessness in their own state.

Since 1980, Iowa's poverty rate has risen steadily, along with the number of homeless poor. While we don't have an accurate figure for the number of homeless in Des Moines, Iowa, we know for certain that the city's sheltered homeless population has increased by 46 to 58 percent since 1984.[17] According to a survey of shelter providers, the number of those in need of shelter exceeds the number of available beds. They stated that they must turn away homeless people. The lack of shelter for the mentally ill, women, and families seems to be the most critical.

As in other parts of the country, numerous factors contribute to the increase in homeless people in Des Moines. Some of the factors are prevalent throughout the country, while others are unique to Iowa.

One common factor is the scarcity of low-income housing. In the last twenty years, urban renewal programs changed many American cities, and Des Moines was not spared. As the country began to rebuild its cities in the 1970s, low-income housing units were torn down or renovated to become higher-income housing units. The median rent for Des Moines increased by 47 percent between 1980

– 34

and 1985. Concurrently, the federal government stopped subsidizing new low-income housing and sharply reduced its level of support for building new low-income units. The resulting shortages in public housing are dramatic. Thousands of people are on waiting lists for public housing, and the wait is usually over five years.[18]

The second major cause of homelessness in Iowa is the rising cost of utilities, along with the inadequate level of support for Aid to Families with Dependent Children (AFDC).

Since 1979, the cost of electricity in Iowa has increased by 66.4 percent, and the cost of gas has risen by 131.7 percent. A survey conducted by the state found that utility costs ranked second only to unemployment as the major cause of hunger.[19]

AFDC is a federal social welfare program administered by the states and counties. The program originated as part of the Social Security Act of 1935. In Iowa, as in other states, eligibility is based on the deprivation of children, due to incapacity or unemployment of either or both parents. From 1980 to 1985, the number of cases increased by over 6 percent. But despite inflation and rising costs over that period, a family of three received $300 in 1980 and $326 in 1985. Their purchasing power was cut by nearly one-fourth.[20]

Thirdly, there is a severe lack of community services for the mentally ill, resulting in an untold number of street people in need of medical attention. Like AFDC recipients, the mentally ill, usually unemployed, also receive government assistance, which has not kept up with the rising cost of rent and utilities. As a result, an increasing number of the mentally ill are homeless because they cannot pay for housing. In Iowa it is estimated that less than one-third of the mentally ill in need of housing are receiving assistance in community residential facilities.

The degree to which the farm crisis has contributed to the homeless situation is not clear. However, the poverty rate

*As part of a bank's foreclosure
on a Michigan farm in 1985, an
auctioneer (foreground) calls
for bids on a tractor, as the
owner sits astride it. The farm
had been in the family for
four generations.*

in Iowa has risen sharply as farm families experience enormous financial problems and, as a result, lose their farms and their homes. It was estimated that by 1986 about one-third of Iowa's farmers would face bankruptcy or lose their farms.[21] While most farmers have not become homeless, because they have doubled up with other family members or found refuge in trailers, farm workers are faced with massive unemployment, which could eventually lead to homelessness.

Des Moines, Iowa's largest city, has a population of almost two hundred thousand. In 1980, 10.6 percent of the city's population were living below the official poverty level. (This figure was not as bad as the national poverty rate of 12.4 percent.) By 1983 the percentage of Americans living below the poverty level had risen to 15.2. In Iowa by 1983, according to the state income tax returns, 13 percent of the population were below the poverty level, a figure considered extremely conservative because it does not take into account tax returns of people who had no income or those whose income was too low to be taxed. According to the Bureau of Labor Statistics, the unemployment rate in Des Moines was 7 percent in 1984, over 8 percent by 1985, and has risen steadily since.[22]

So, as we can see, as unemployment rises steadily and rent and utility costs increase dramatically, the crisis of becoming homeless is unquestionably the next step.

By 1985 the national delinquency rate for all mortgages rose to a record high. In Iowa during the same period, the number of evictions rose to a staggering 126 percent, a further indication that a large number of people could not keep up with rising costs and could not pay their rent.[23]

In 1984 approximately 400 shelter beds were available in Des Moines. By 1985 the number of beds had increased to 650, but the shelters still had to turn away homeless people. Both privately and federally funded shelters in Des Moines charged between four and nine dollars per night for a bed, making them unaffordable for the most destitute homeless people. In the course of one year, the homeless population had increased by over 50 percent.[24]

Like other areas that denied the obvious and documented shelter crisis, the city and the state did not step in to fill the gap. Instead, churches and community groups provided services that some people still consider to be the responsibility of government.

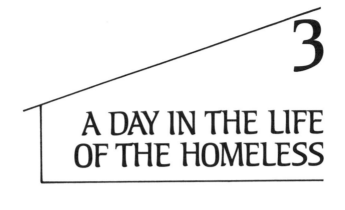

3

A DAY IN THE LIFE
OF THE HOMELESS

Perhaps the most significant fact about the homeless is that they are not a homogeneous group. They are very different from one another.

The homeless who are mentally ill and live on the streets are different from the homeless who live in shantytowns in Portland, Oregon. By pooling their resources these people have been able to live in a semicommunity. They have developed a bond, based on their homeless status. Women and children living in New York City's welfare hotels are different from those people who are in search of shelter daily. The people who sleep on cots in church basements tend to be different from those sleeping in large city shelters, most of whom are young black and Hispanic men without long histories of serious mental illness. They all have one thing in common, however. They are all homeless.

Betty, a heavyset black woman, lives outside a fancy ice-cream parlor on the Upper East Side of Manhattan. She is there every day. She wears three or four layers of clothes, is covered by a blanket, and has bags all around her. Her hair is matted because it has not been combed for weeks or perhaps months. Her legs are very swollen, and her clothes are dirty and don't fit her. She talks to herself and always stays in front of this same restaurant, even on the coldest winter nights.

I approached her holding my breath, because the smell emanating from her was vile. I was reminded of another homeless woman who told me that she smelled bad to keep men from raping her.

"Are you okay, Betty?" I asked her on a day when the temperature had dropped to ten degrees, with winds gusting to thirty miles an hour. The thought of her lying on the sidewalk in such bitterly cold weather concerned me. I had on two sweaters and a winter coat and I still felt chilled.

"Why you call me Betty, when you know that my name is Fannie?"

Worried that I might be from the government, trying to make her move, she got angry and told me to leave her alone: "The next time when you come, knock before you come in my house."

Betty (or Fannie, as she sometimes likes to be called) considers this spot her home. It is her spot in the world. She has no belongings except for the items she has in her plastic bags. She is a regular fixture between the bank and the ice-cream parlor. She eats what people give her, and sometimes she ventures to the garbage can a few feet away, but only when no one is looking, because she is afraid that someone may take "her" spot. When she is in a good mood, she sings and talks about her children. She doesn't seem to recognize people from one day to the next, but even that may not be true. That may be her defense for living on the streets. Fannie/Betty is typical of the homeless mentally ill now living on the streets without proper medication. It is very possible that she may be a former mental patient. It is certain that she has lost touch with reality as we perceive it. However, she has managed to survive against the worst odds. She eats whatever the restaurant throws out, what she can find in the garbage, or what passersby offer her.

Once, she had been missing from her spot for a few days. When she returned I asked her if the police had forced her to go into a shelter, a policy enforced by several cities when the temperature falls below freezing.

"You're trying to confuse me," she responded angrily. "I was busy. I went to see my sister."

At that point, I felt it would be better to change the subject: "Can I get you some coffee?"

"I got some. Can't you see?" She was drinking from a cup that had seen better days and had probably been given to her hours ago by a stranger.

"Shouldn't she be getting supervised care?" I asked a worker at a program for the homeless. "Don't you do any outreach?"

His answer was predictable: "We can't. We're at capacity. Sometimes, in the summer, when we have fewer people, we can reach out more aggressively, but we couldn't possibly handle any more people now then we already have in the program."

When the program staffers do go on the streets in search of the mentally ill homeless, they often concentrate on Grand Central Station, because a large number of the homeless, about fifteen hundred, make it their home. The possibility of a social worker or an outreach group coming across Fannie and succeeding in placing her in a protective environment is difficult to calculate.

There are many like her on the streets and they are the hardest to help. They won't go into city shelters because they will be even more abused there than on the street. Because church shelters are usually staffed by volunteers, many of them cannot accommodate people in need of professional help. They need a residential community program and those that exist have few vacancies.

The First Moravian Church in New York City has been a pioneer in helping the homeless. They maintain a twenty-four-hour drop-in center, where church workers feed three meals a day to over two hundred people. From the center, city buses take the homeless every night to the various churches and synagogues where beds are provided.

*Left: a homeless woman in
New York's Greenwich Village.
Above: at the First Moravian Church in
New York City, a woman waits for the bus
that will take her to a shelter for the night.*

I visited the center one rainy Saturday evening. The homeless at the Moravian Church are lucky. The people in this program know that at least they'll eat, that they'll probably stay at a church shelter during the night, and that they'll sleep in peace without fear of being mugged or abused. They can take showers every day and get clean clothes, even if the clothes are not the correct size. The church has more than enough clothes to give away. This is because homeless people can't take clothes that they don't wear because they can't lug them from place to place.

The homeless at this church are all adults. Women with children are not accepted, and there are strict rules about age eligibility. The center won't admit people under thirty unless they have a psychiatric problem, but they will refer people in need of serious psychiatric help to other facilities, such as Saint Francis. The people in charge of the center monitor those in need of medication; they provide a medical examination for all those coming into the program; and they make sure that a person is deloused, if need be, before they send him or her to a church for the night. "If you got to be homeless," said one of the men," this is one of the best places to be."

There, watching people waiting to be taken by a bus to a shelter for that night, I could see the different types of homeless people. About 30 percent of them are on some type of medication for mental illness, to control their behavior and enable them to function at least marginally. If they forget to take their medication—and many do—a staff member will remind them. The church takes responsibility for their medication if they can't handle it.

Some men patiently played cards while they waited to leave. Some sat at the same table with others but kept to themselves. Some muttered to themselves, while others watched television. One very heavyset man was listening to music from a Walkman and was busily writing on a pad. I thought he might be a reporter, but I was informed that he was waiting to go into a shelter.

"I don't see my name on the list. Which shelter am I going to?" asked a woman with a noticeable limp. Another man approached with a long story, asking why he couldn't go to the shelter to which he was assigned. The staff member, who has been working with people like these for four years, showed no impatience or irritation, but responded calmly to their needs.

He explained, "We put up a list of names and places where they'll be going for the night. They come in and check the list. Then, if anyone is not on the list, we try to accommodate them if we have the room."

"Does everyone have a place to go sleep?" I asked. The answer was an expected no. It's not until almost seven in the evening that some people know if they have a shelter where they can sleep or if they have to stay at the Moravian Church, which has only hard chairs to sleep on. Fortunately, most people are accommodated. The staff decides, based on numerous factors, how to allocate the church beds available at the different locations. Those who are on medication, are disabled or elderly, or for some other reason seem to be in the greatest need, get first priority for bed space. Some people on the list don't arrive on time for the bus, so they lose their place. On this particular night, almost everyone found a shelter.

It reminded me of leaving for sleep-away camp. They were treated a bit like children. The buses arrived, and the staff tried to match the names of those going to one facility or another with an original list of names that is constantly changing as the homeless request one shelter over a previous one.

"I just came from the doctor. He said that my blood pressure is very high, very high," one man emphasized. "They can't give me medication till they finish all the tests. So I can't go to the shelter that you have me down for because it's too hot there. I want to go to the one in Brooklyn."

The staff member, without much inquiry, took his

*Homeless men boarding a bus to be
taken to a church-sponsored shelter*

name off one list, placed it on the other, and took another man off that list. A woman came over to give the staffer a kiss because he had placed her at her "favorite" shelter. Another man was still not on any list, and the time was getting short. "Come on, send me to Saint Ignatius," he begged. Shaking his head, the staffer said, "I can't. There is no room there." Eventually, they found him a place because, fortunately, another man hadn't shown up.

"They go through this every day, not knowing if or where they'll find shelter?" I wondered aloud. The staff member nodded with a smile and said, "We usually do find a place for them. And we do try to accommodate their preferences whenever we can."

It appeared that was the best they could do. The others, left without a bed, braced themselves for the night. The few remaining chose to sleep at the Moravian Church instead of a city shelter because they're afraid of those places.

In the summer, many of the same people prefer to sleep on the streets or in the parks, so the church then has a smaller homeless population to care for. Ironically, it is during these months that in some programs staff members go out to bring in people staying on the streets.

So, this is the best of how the homeless live. Yet even under these circumstances, their lives are a daily struggle— not knowing where they'll sleep, or if there will be room for them, or if someone else will get ahead on the list because that person is deemed more needy. They confront this situation daily.

One of the homeless men, whose sleeping bag had been stolen, was ready with a solution. He said, "So I'll live in my cardboard condominium. It's not bad. With your body heat you won't freeze to death, even if you cut a couple of holes to breathe." Many of the homeless sleep in cardboard packing boxes from large appliances such as refrigerators and washing machines. They place them over a grate, and the heat coming from below keeps them warm. Apparently, weekends are bad because fewer deliveries take place, and fewer cardboard boxes are discarded.

Each day, every meal, they search for the next meal. Although now soup kitchens often provide hot meals, many of the homeless routinely go to churches and synagogues for food or to shelters that provide meals at lunchtime.

"How do you know where to go?" I asked a homeless man.

"If you've been on the streets for more than a few days, you get to know where the places are. You talk to the others on the streets and they give you some information."

Others live on garbage or money received from returning cans and bottles to stores or donating blood—even if disease-ridden—which is always good for quick cash. Some of them are entrepreneurial. They take their uneaten food, such as half a sandwich, from the shelter and sell it on the streets. One woman kept going back to a shelter that provides Pampers for babies—with the same note from a social worker, which she tried to use repeatedly to get additional Pampers—so that she could sell them to other women on the streets or in the welfare hotels. "Homeless people will try to sell anything," commented a formerly homeless woman. "It's survival."

If one factor characterizes homelessness, it is the uncertainty of waiting in line. Getting food means waiting in very long lines, as does securing a bed, particularly in city shelters. Getting any form of government assistance means standing in line. Planning ahead or the notion that there is something beyond today is a luxury that the homeless do not know. They live one day at a time.

A homeless man
with his dogs

Whereas the shopping cart used to be symbolic of the supermarket, today it is often associated with homelessness, as many of the homeless use shopping carts to hold their possessions.

The homeless also have a disproportionate number of illness, including AIDS, pneumonia, tuberculosis, malnutrition, dental problems, and infections. Many have serious problems with their legs because of the tremendous amount of standing and walking they do without proper rest. Most have not had medical attention for many years. There are those with drug and alcohol abuse problems that often lead to other illnesses, including liver disease and hepatitis. Some homeless women have been raped and are pregnant, yet they are not aware of it.

"The longer someone stays homeless, the more they deteriorate," commented a nurse who treats the homeless. That certainly stands to reason. If people are homeless for a long time, showers become fewer and fewer, and their general health deteriorates. They also begin to lose touch with the norms of society; what dominates their thinking is the search for food and shelter.

Some people have suggested that the homeless are homeless because they have mental problems. But after spending time with the homeless as well as those who have worked with these people for a long time, I realized that even if a person were perfectly healthy when he or she became homeless, the despair, the fear, the never-ending search for food and shelter, the vile smell of the body, the deterioration of the mind, and the lack of what we associate with a civilized life would drive anyone crazy. It is no wonder that some of the homeless don't want to talk. They are abused by people on the streets. They are treated poorly at many shelters. They cannot find their way in the bureaucratic maze of the government assistance programs. Often they find themselves totally alone, fighting against waves of despair.

I wonder how other cities, particularly those that have a reputation for handling their affairs in an orderly way, tackle their homeless problem.

In a recent poll, Pittsburgh was voted the most livable

city in America. Public officials boast about the success of handling their homeless problem. I went to Pittsburgh to see how their shelters operate.

"We have six thousand homeless in this city, and we have six thousand beds where they can sleep," I was told by a journalist who had spent a night impersonating a homeless woman at Bethlehem Haven, a shelter for women.

I visited Bethlehem Haven, which is located in the basement of a large church in the center of the city. The program, religious in orientation, operates in a warm and friendly place that provides food and shelter on a nightly basis. The people who run the program don't ask questions, nor do they make judgments about their "guests," or "ladies," as they prefer to call them. Their purpose is to provide food and shelter.

By eight o'clock in the evening, the women began to line up outside the shelter. Volunteers have donated food and set up tables for the "ladies" so they can sit down to a warm meal, often the only one they will have eaten that day. After supper the women take a shower; then they are assigned beds, which are placed close together, dormitory style. They each have a blanket, a pillow, and clean sheets. Bethlehem Haven is the kind of shelter that many women return to every night, so the regulars have their own beds, where they leave some personal belongings.

Some women talk to each other as they eat, but most of them keep to themselves. Sometimes they mutter to themselves as they prepare for the night. The women are given nightgowns to sleep in, and while they sleep, the volunteers wash and dry their clothes, a gesture certainly unique to Bethlehem Haven. In the morning, after a hot breakfast, they must leave the premises, because the children from the church nursery school come to play in the same area.

Some of the women have been coming there since it opened in 1982; some have their own bed where they sleep every night, while others come for a night or a few nights until they find a permanent place to stay.

Very little is known about some of them. There is no pressure to talk. There are no social workers or psychologists. It is a place of hospitality. It is a church, and those in charge view their mission as helping the poor and the more unfortunate who are down on their luck. But the staff know some of their "guests," and whenever they can, they try to help them get in touch with other programs that can provide services for them. Like the Moravian Church in New York, the Haven performs a very important function. They permit the women to use the church as their address, which means they can at least begin the process of getting government assistance. They can become eligible for welfare and food stamps. Then they can start the difficult process of finding a place to live.

The major difference between Pittsburgh and New York City is Pittsburgh's success in finding permanent housing for the homeless. In Pittsburgh I talked with several formerly homeless women who, after a brief period of homelessness, found permanent apartments they could afford. In a city like New York, it is virtually impossible for people on public assistance to pay rent with their allotment from the government.

According to Dr. Ellen Bassuk, associate professor of psychiatry at Harvard Medical School, all homeless people are depressed and anxious. She has observed that being homeless erodes people's self-esteem. "It makes them invisible without any real identity." She further suggests that they don't have the usual connectedness to other people and to institutions. They are isolated and estranged. "They are regularly assaulted; the women are regularly raped. So their depression is at a much more profound level than most people's. . . . Everybody should imagine what it would be like to lose absolutely everything so that you don't even have somebody to call up."[25]

I looked through some of the records of the homeless at the Moravian Church, and I was reminded of her comments. The questionnaire that each "guest" is asked to complete provides a line for the name of "the person to call in an emergency." On most of the questionnaires the line was left blank. Perhaps this statement tells a small part of the story.

As one reporter commented, "It's a reporter's job to use ingenuity to find and touch human life on the edge. But it was tough to walk away from them and back to our warm houses." I totally shared her feelings.

4
SEARCHING
FOR SHELTER

It was a bitterly cold Saturday night in New York City. The wind was blowing, the temperature was nearly ten degrees, and the leftover snow and sleet turned the streets into sheets of ice. I went to a neighborhood church that offers shelter for the homeless on Saturday and Sunday nights. This church is part of a coalition of over 125 churches and synagogues that have formed an organization, Partnership for the Homeless, to provide food and shelter.

In the church basement, beds that looked as if they were once army cots were lined up next to each other. The volunteers had placed a towel, a blanket, and a clean sheet on each bed. Since the "guests" were coming from the First Moravian Church, they had already eaten dinner, so we put out cookies, some fruit, and hot coffee. Twelve people were expected. Some were regulars, but others were coming for the first time. It is the job of the volunteer coordinator to make sure that everything is ready when the "guests" arrive at approximately eight o'clock at night, transported to this church by a city bus.

Considering the circumstances, a fairly cheery group arrived. For people spending this night in the basement of a church, all in one room in dormitory style, they were more upbeat then I had expected. But of course this was a fairly lucky group. They came from the Moravian Church, which has a long history of caring for the homeless, and among places to stay, this was a prime shelter for a homeless person.

The place was clean, and the beds were spread out spaciously, unlike some city shelters, where more than a thousand people occupy one room. Fortunately, in this church, only twelve people had to sleep in one room. Imagine, if you can, a city shelter—a gigantic room that serves as a place to sleep or, more accurately, a place to stay—inside an armory or gymnasium, for as many as 2,000 people.

As the "guests" got off the bus, Katherine, the chief volunteer, greeted everyone warmly. Recognizing some of them, she gave me a little background about each person. They put their suitcases or bags on their beds. (The regulars have their own beds, and everyone respected their claims for specific beds.)

This particular night, we had a tall black man—a regular who was lively and talkative—and an Asian man, dressed in a jacket and tie, who immediately lay down on a bed in the farthest corner of the basement and spoke to no one. A black couple came with a suitcase filled with neatly folded clothing. They both changed into pajamas, almost making it seem as if they were at home. Some people went to bed immediately, while others sat around the table, drinking coffee and smoking cigarettes.

One of the volunteers quietly said to the men who were chain-smoking, "Cigarettes are not good for your health." One of the men jokingly replied, "I can't imagine that being homeless is good for my health."

"Did you see the *New York Post* today?" a middle-aged white man turned to me and asked.

"No," I responded. "Why, what was in the paper?"

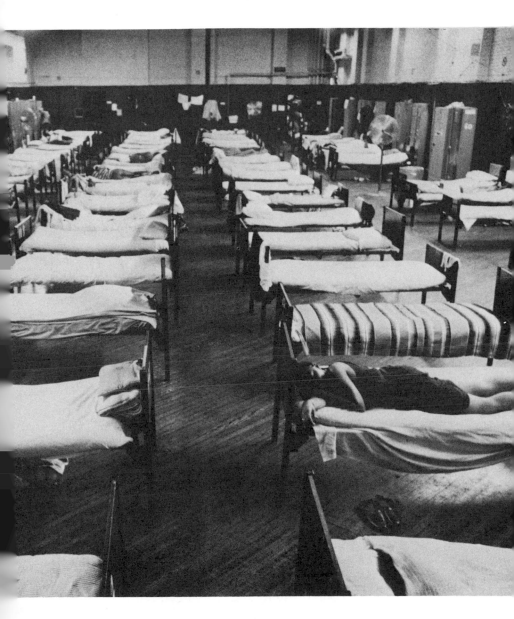

*A city shelter for homeless women
in New York City*

Another white man, dressed in a clean white shirt and a tie, as if he had just come from work, answered the question. "Mayor Koch went to Poland and told those people that there were no homeless people in New York. Can you imagine telling those people that we have no homeless?"

"So what are we?" chuckled a heavyset older white man.

"We got locked out," joked the man with the white shirt.

"This coffee is good," one man said to another.

A white woman in her thirties turned to me and asked if I was a volunteer or "with us." The question stunned me for a moment. Then I realized that we didn't look that different. She asked her next question: "Is there any sugar?" There were pounds of sugar. The "guests" put plenty of it into their coffee, not knowing when they would have sugar again.

The lights went out by ten o'clock. Lights out at ten on a Saturday night? I wondered why so early. The answer was obvious long before ten. These homeless people were exhausted. Walking the streets all day, every day, searching for a place to sleep, is a physically exhausting experience.

Slim, a tall man, kept the conversation going, but even his energy was fading. "He won't be with us for very much longer, I don't think," said my guide, the volunteer coordinator. "He got his check from the government for his disability, and I think he'll take that money and go down south." Slim had children in this area, but they didn't know that he was homeless. They thought he still lived in an SRO hotel. What happened to Slim has happened to thousands of others. He lived in a hotel that was converted into luxury condominiums. He couldn't find a place to stay for long, and he didn't want his children to know he was homeless. He left the few belongings he had at a relative's place, and he has been staying in shelters ever since.

Around the table, the conversation seemed ordinary.

After the "guests" got over Mayor Koch's comment about the homeless, they talked about other things. One man, sober, proudly told another that he had stopped drinking for good. Contrary to what some people might believe, the entire group seemed totally sober. None of them appeared to be high on alcohol or drugs, or behaved in a disorderly fashion. They all seemed glad to be inside and glad to be able to put their swollen feet up on a bed. Some chose to keep to themselves, a trait that many of the homeless share. They all looked forward to a relatively restful sleep. They knew that by seven o'clock the next morning, after coffee and doughnuts, they would have to leave and search for the next warm spot. Like most other shelters, this church facility is used for other activities during the day. They had to leave.

Ben, the only one in the group who looked dirty and in need of clean clothes, was the only person who wanted to continue talking. He was a regular. His bed was near the radiator with only one other bed to the side. When he came in, he dropped his plastic bag on his bed so people would know that it was taken.

Crippled, he walks with a pronounced limp. His fingers are noticeably deformed. He yelled across to one of the volunteers, "Hey, I need help with making my bed!" He was young, articulate, and angry, but he was clearly not one of the "crazies," as some of the homeless are called. The look in his eyes indicated that he was very much in control. Ben was also the only one of this group who wanted to tell me how he became homeless. (Many of them feel ashamed and are not comfortable talking about how they got into this situation.)

"That's easy" he said with a bit of arrogance. "I was in the hospital for months with bone cancer," a debilitating disease that gets worse as time goes by. After he was released from the hospital he lost everything. He was in a tremendous amount of pain. Although he was still taking

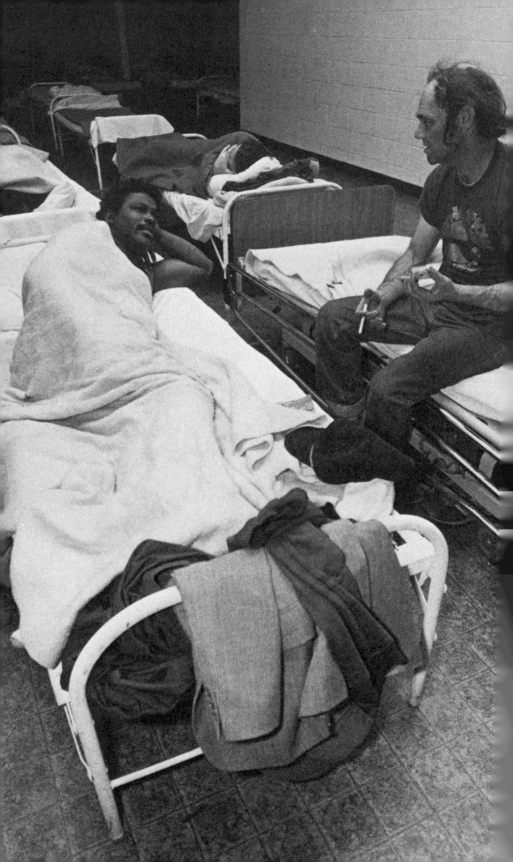

medication, the pain was unbearable. He didn't think he was going to live much longer, so he sought a new way to kill the pain. On the streets he met someone who introduced him to heroin. He quickly became addicted, and he spent all his money buying drugs. Then he started selling drugs to support his habit. But he didn't want to be a drug addict, so he gave up heroin and joined a methadone program. All this time, however, he was still homeless.

According to Ben, he has no family. His mother died; his father remarried a long time ago, and they lost contact. To add to his difficulties, he started having seizures from the combination of the many drugs that he was taking. About a month before I met him, Ben had a seizure in a public restroom, shortly after he had been given some new medication to control seizures. Disoriented, he had no idea where he was or how he got to the hospital. He didn't remember anything.

Ben has been to many shelters and is an expert on which place has the best food. He particularly likes a very prestigious synagogue that serves chicken every night. He eats there regularly and tries to stay at their shelter, but Saturday nights, the synagogue is closed, so he must be elsewhere. He won't go into a city shelter because he has heard too many horror stories about what happens to people in those shelters. He certainly would be a prime target for abuse since he is small, disabled, and sick.

Ben gets some money from the government for his disability, but he says that it is less than $100 a month. He cannot afford an apartment because he has very little money. He cannot work because he is very ill and often in great pain. He was thrown out of one church shelter be-

Homeless men in a Houston,
Texas, Salvation Army
shelter in the winter

cause he had an argument with one of the workers. He had objected to the fact that there were only three showers at the shelter and one of them was never in working order. By the time many of the people showered, the water was no longer hot, and it was hours before he could take a shower.

Ben did seem to be belligerent and angry, and these large facilities are not equipped to handle people who get out of line. After all, they are dealing with hundreds of people in need of food, shelter, a shower, and, in some cases, emergency medical attention. By creating a scene, Ben had not helped his situation. He had one less place to go. He seemed to be the only ungrateful person in the group, unimpressed by what the churches had done for the homeless. He was aware of all the money the churches received from the city, so he felt the least they could do was fix the showers. According to him, even when the showers worked, they were dirty. Needless to say, with only two showers available, after hundreds of homeless people cleaned themselves, the showers were probably *very* dirty.

According to the church staff, Ben is typical of the homeless who want to be left alone, won't follow rules, and cannot be a part of a group. They keep to themselves rather than adhere to rules and regulations.

"One day, I just couldn't take it any more," he said. "I took all the money I had and went into the YMCA. That was great. I was all by myself. I could no longer deal with all these people and all the noise. I spent the whole day lying in bed. But you can't do that but once in a blue moon. It is so expensive."

As he spoke about that one day alone, saying that all he wanted was a warm place, with a shower and a bed and quiet, it seemed pitiful to me that a man who may be dying should be spending his last days searching for shelter and food. He seemed to have very few belongings. His most important posession, his medication, was kept in his coat pocket. He knew that it was in his best interests to keep his important possessions on his person to prevent their being stolen, a normal occurrence in most city shelters.

I wondered why a social worker couldn't find a place for him to stay after he left the hospital. According to Ben, when he left the hospital, he went into a hotel, or SRO type of room, for a while, but he got heavily into drugs, didn't have money, and quickly found himself living on the streets and in shelters. Now he is trying to rebuild his life. Of course, that's his side of the story. Others claim that Ben simply won't follow instructions or rules, and the price of independence is living this way. He won't show up for appointments and loses forms that he should fill out in order to get help.

This neighborhood church is only one of hundreds of churches and synagogues that serve as shelters for the homeless. They offer little beyond the basics. Usually the shelter is in the basement or the children's day-care room. For the homeless, these facilities are a luxury. They are at least safe places to stay, places where they can sleep without fear of losing their few belongings, and places that have warm, friendly volunteers who try to make them feel like guests.

However, because these churches and synagogues make up only a small portion of the shelters, and because some are open only on weekends or only on certain weekdays, many of the homeless must go into the city shelters, sleep in train stations and bus depots, or stay on the streets. Still, the number of private facilities has grown enormously, just as the number of homeless has grown. The Partnership for the Homeless has worked hard to get people involved in this issue, and to persuade private organizations to open their doors to the homeless. In New York City alone, the Partnership has over 100 facilities offering shelter and food to the homeless. But it takes an enormous amount of time and energy to organize these volunteer operations. The church that housed only those twelve people required two volunteers—one male and one female—to stay overnight

with the "guests." They are in constant need of volunteers. It is not that difficult to get a volunteer to help one night, but to find a volunteer who will agree to help out a few nights a month is another matter: "A lot of people try it once, but they can't take it. It depresses them too much," said one of the volunteer coordinators.

When I left the church, I realized that I had never felt happier going home to my warm apartment, thinking of all those people I had met who were spending their day looking for, and hoping they could find, a warm shelter for another night. Tuesday is the same as Monday—each night securing a place to stay, getting on line in the afternoon to have a place at night, getting on soup lines in order to eat, waiting in line to take a shower, standing in line to get on the bus provided by the city to get to the church—all for one night's rest.

Jack Coleman, a well-known former college president, and Pat Harper, an award-winning television anchorwoman, both lived the life of a homeless person for a few days and nights. They seemed shattered by the experience. They both said that if there is a hell, living this way must be it. Yet these people who did get a closer look at the life of the homeless did it for only a few days. They knew that at any time they could stop their impersonation and go home. But the homeless cannot go home. They cannot stop when they get tired of living this way. Most of the homeless have been living this way for years. It is amazing that they don't give

A homeless woman stands with her possessions in front of Grand Central Station in New York City. To the right is an advertisement for the Bowery Bank that reads, "Have it all when you retire."

– 65

up. Maybe just a day at the YMCA, where they can find peace and solitude for a few hours, renews their spirit and gives them the strength to keep going. Or maybe it is the hope that this way of living will end soon, and they will again have a place they can call home.

When I left the church I wondered for a moment about taking them all home for the day. It was so cold outside that I felt guilty not offering them my warm home. But then I thought, What about tomorrow, and the day after tomorrow, and the day after that? They need a permanent home, not a temporary place to stay. They need permanent solutions, not charity.

As Robert Hayes, president of the Coalition for the Homeless, put it, "The problem of the homeless is that they need housing, housing, and housing." The volunteers can provide warmth and compassion. They can provide shelter and food for the night. They can't provide housing. Only the federal, state, and city governments can provide that.

CHILDREN
WITHOUT HOMES

On my visit to an after-school program that provides services for homeless children, I asked, "What's it like to be homeless?" The children, all trying to help me find an answer to this question, ranged from eight to twelve in age.

I imagine that being homeless is a nightmare, but being homeless with a child must be total hell. Yet, according to all statistics, it is this group—families—that is the fastest-growing number of homeless. They now constitute 21 percent of the homeless nationally. One out of every five homeless people has a family.[26]

It is difficult to try to understand the way the city of New York deals with homeless people with children. It seems to make no sense at all. Because the city destroyed a great many buildings that once housed the poor, these people now have no place to live, so the city places them in dingy, run-down, roach- and often rat-infested hotels. Many of these hotels are in the high-crime, midtown area, away from parks or schools.

In most of these hotels there are only single rooms, with no cooking facilities. Often, the rooms do not have private baths, but, instead, there is one bathroom in the hallway for an entire floor. These hotels are crime-ridden, and drugs, prostitution, and even muggings are commonplace. The homeless parents who are sent to these hotels with their children fear for their children and for themselves. The most ironic aspect of this arrangement is that the city uses its funds for emergency shelter to pay hotel landlords exorbitant sums of money—sometimes as much as $2,000 a month for a room. Some hotels are making huge profits housing the homeless in terrible conditions. And some homeless families have lived in these hotels for several years.

The city also gives these families a "restaurant allowance" so that they can eat in restaurants or use the money to eat in one of the shelters. Thus, the city spends much more money feeding and housing these homeless families than it would if permanent shelters were built. But the Reagan administration reduced federal funding for building new low-income housing, thereby throwing the burden onto the cities, which are often financially unable to assume the responsibility.

Under the Reagan administration, federal housing assistance dropped drastically, from $29 billion in 1980 to less than $8 billion in 1986. And today, New York City is paying the price of a luxury apartment to house families in SRO welfare hotels.

More than 340,000 apartments previously renting for under $400 a month are now priced out of reach for most families. We should add to this picture that 67 percent of

A child stands alone in a grimy corridor of one of New York City's welfare hotels. The city pays as much as $2,000 a month to house a family in a one-room, rodent-infested, crime-ridden hotel.

New York households earn less than $25,000 a year, and 50 percent earn less than $15,000 a year—startling figures for a rich city.[27] So, when a family becomes homeless because of fire, building demolition or renovation, nonpayment of rent, or any other reason, it is a tough struggle to find a new place to live. It is nearly impossible to find an affordable apartment, particularly if the family in question is a single-parent household headed by a mother caring for her children. If she is on welfare, the rent allowance is approximately $247 per month, far below the standard costs of apartments in most major cities. In addition, most landlords require a minimum of one month's rent and a one-month security deposit upon signing of the lease. Because of this, thousands of families live in welfare hotels, waiting to find a permanent apartment they can afford.

Some of the teachers at New York City public schools are used to the sight of children coming to school and falling asleep at their desks. These children don't sleep at night because the hotels are so noisy or because they share one room with many brothers and sisters, some of whom are infants who cry all night. The teachers also suspect that many of these children ask for seconds at lunch because they probably didn't have dinner the night before. As one teacher observed, "These kids have problems you can't even imagine. Being in school is the best thing in their lives. If they were here more, we could help them more."

In New York City almost 11,000 children, 6,000 of whom are of school age, live in hotels and shelters for the homeless. As one would expect, many of these children attend school irregularly. And when they do attend, they have a very difficult time paying attention and catching up with what they missed. To make matters worse, the schools are usually not located near the hotels, and the children often have to be bused from other parts of town. According to school records, some children regularly miss one or two days a week, while others simply drop out of sight for long periods of time.

Most of these homeless families, particularly those headed by single women, have a very difficult time coping. Often, a mother must raise several children in one room, without a kitchen, with a bathroom down the hall, with no place for the children to play except in the hallways and the lobby. All kinds of crimes occur in front of these children, and often they get involved in carrying drugs and committing crimes themselves. To go to school and pay attention under such conditions seems an almost impossible task. As one homeless mother of three put it, "Living like this, it kills you."

Families who have recently become homeless sometimes move a dozen times before a semipermanent hotel room is found. The children might miss school for weeks at a time before they have a place to stay for more than a few nights. As the mother of one such homeless family stated, "We've been in the Bronx. We've been in Staten Island. One night they send me to a hotel in the Bronx, then I have to come back here the next day, and then they send me back there. How do you keep a child in school with this?" According to school officials, the children are often a year or two behind in their grade and are often labeled "emotionally disturbed" or "retarded." It would be no surprise if many of these children became wards of the state.

At a very early age, the children know hunger and a nomadic life without roots, no place that they can call their own, no place to invite a friend. No one can say what it means to grow up without roots. But most psychologists agree that it is important for children to have continuity, a place where they feel comfortable, without worrying about hunger and shelter. They need stability. Instead, at an early age, these children have seen and experienced things that most adults never see.

While most of the hotels in the Times Square area are horrifying, some of the others are a bit more "civilized." And, though the rooms are small and a family of four may have to share one room and fold the cots so that someone can get through to the bathroom, some of the children are remarkably resilient despite their adversity.

Boys Harbor, in New York City, has a special program for homeless children. Founded in 1937 by Anthony Drexel Duke, from a wealthy family, the program is underwritten by city, state, and private funds. Watching the children here gave me a glimmer of hope. The city sends a bus to some of the hotels after school to pick up the children and take them to Boys Harbor, an old converted building that was formerly a school. At Boys Harbor, the children are supervised by teachers and are able to take part in many different activities. They can do their homework, which they often can't do in hotel rooms that are usually crowded with other family members. And they get help from a teacher. They are also offered dinner before they are returned by bus to their hotels for the night.

Here they have a place where they can run and play, and since most of the children come from the same hotels, they know each other, make friends, and have some sense of regularity and normalcy in their lives.

At Boys Harbor I met Henry, a very alert but shy boy, about nine years old, and we started to talk about being homeless. He listened patiently. He agreed that being homeless must be really awful. A bit puzzled, he asked me why we were talking about the homeless, because he didn't know very much about being homeless.

"You don't consider yourself homeless?" I asked naively.

"No," he replied, a bit confused. "I live in a hotel."

I later realized that none of the children considered themselves homeless. They live in hotels. Being homeless, to them, is living on the streets. So, once we defined our terms, we were able to talk about how they came to live in hotels.

Many of the children said that they had lived in very bad conditions before they moved to the hotels. Many were poor, living in buildings that were badly maintained or not kept up at all, but at least they had a couple of rooms. Many of them had experienced fires in their apartments, and some said that they really didn't know why they moved to the hotels, except that their mother could not afford to pay the rent any longer so they had to move. In the beginning, some of them had stayed with other family members for a night or two. Then, they remembered moving from one place to another until they finally arrived at a particular hotel. Most of them had been living there for months or even years.

"What is the worst thing about living in a hotel?" I asked a very verbal twelve-year-old who was then living in a comparatively decent hotel.

Without hesitation, he replied, "You have no privacy. Everyone is yelling and screaming. My baby sister cries at night. My mother tries to warm up her bottle at night on a hot plate [illegal in that hotel because of inadequate wiring]. I can't sleep at night. So I'm tired when I have to get up and go to school. Then, you can't have any friends over. They make fun of us so I don't tell anyone where I live. The kids at Boys Harbor are my only friends. The [hotel] is like living in the zoo."

"Do you have any toys?" I asked him.

"I got a few from people who donated toys to the homeless at Christmas. There's no place to play with them, and there's no place to put them in the room."

Many of the children also complained that when they go back to the hotels, they usually find their mothers depressed and short-tempered. So not only do they have to live with little sleep, without friends, without beds they can call their own, and in fear of being mugged, but also their mothers—usually their only parents—have little patience or energy to give them. Very often, after years of living in hotels, the mothers give up trying to find a permanent place to live. They don't know where to look anymore, so they settle for an existence that takes an enormous toll on everyone.

– 73

The children find themselves further and further behind in school. They cannot concentrate and have difficulty paying attention because they are tired. Aside from special places like Boys Harbor, which serves only a few hotels, the children have no place to play, no place to do homework, no place to develop friendships. Their lives are nomadic, and there is little that they can count on. They have few possessions they can call their own. They all hope for a larger place to live, but many express real doubt that it will happen soon.

"What do you miss the most?" I asked one of the girls.

"I want a cat. But I can't have one now."

Another child said, "I had a dog, but I had to give her up. We have no place for a dog. As soon as we have a place, I want to have her back. I loved her."

Although most of the children were not sure why they were in their predicament, none of them blamed their parents for it. They all believed that their mothers were trying to find a better place, but it was difficult and it would take some time. And, in spite of their bad fortune, most of the children at Boys Harbor were well behaved and energetic. Getting away from their environment was one of the best things that had happened to them.

As one of the teachers commented, "I personally think we should do special programs and spend the money. In the long run, it will save dollars. These kids would get an education and not just drop out and become wards of the state later."

Special programs like the one offered by Boys Harbor may indeed be the brightest spots in the lives of some of these children. Such programs offer them a place where they can be children and do the things that children do: play, have friends, do homework, and eat dinner regularly.

With all the problems they face, it would be a miracle if the hotel children grew up to be healthy, competent individuals, prepared to enter society in a productive way. They experience undue hardship and poverty, and the temptation to enter a life of crime is hard to resist. Since they have missed so much time, many of them will be lucky to finish school. Living conditions in welfare hotels are not conducive to concentrating on schoolwork.

Some people deny that such children should be classified as homeless at all, since technically speaking they have roofs over their heads. Without a doubt, there is a difference between living in a hotel room and living in a cardboard box on the cold streets or in the bathroom of a train or bus station. But living without a permanent home is taking its toll on these children, in ways that may not show up or be fully understood for many years to come. The only hope is to shorten their period of homelessness and, while they are in hotels, to develop programs like Boys Harbor that can help them through this period.

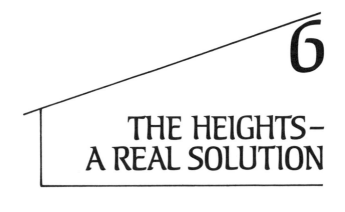

6
THE HEIGHTS–
A REAL SOLUTION

The Heights was one of the most encouraging places that I visited, especially after hearing so many stories of pain and disappointment, of lives that seemed permanently impaired, without happy endings, and after visiting shelters filled with violence, anger, and desperation.

The Heights, located on the Upper West Side of Manhattan in New York City, is a home for fifty five people who had previously lived on the streets or in shelters. They were fortunate to be the lucky few who were accepted into this model SRO.

The Heights is simply an older building that was renovated and painted and is now one of the best-maintained buildings in a lower-income neighborhood. The project took many years to bring to fruition, but its existence is testimony to the fact that we must find permanent solutions to the problem of temporary shelters.

Among the people who live at the Heights are former mental patients, alcoholics, and drug addicts. Some are on medication. Others were burned out of their apartments. One resident was a teenage runaway who is now attending college. Some lived on the streets for long periods of time, others lived in shelters, some came from other temporary residential facilities. They are the few lucky ones who were either known by those who developed the Heights—social workers who had encountered these people on the streets—or were referred by temporary shelters. The people who live at the Heights are a diverse group. Fifteen of the residents have a history of mental illness and, because they have some difficulties in coping with their everyday lives, are assisted by social workers. The age range of the residents is from eighteen to elderly. The Heights is totally integrated —there are black, white and Hispanic residents of both sexes.

Upon entering the building, you are greeted by the person at the front desk, who asks that you sign the guest book. Then, by means of a buzzer system, you pass through another door and into the main part of the house. The first thing you notice is that it is impeccably clean. The floors shine and signs on the wall request that people put their cigarettes in ashtrays. Off the entranceway, a large dining room, with flowers on the piano, creates a real community feeling.

"Do all the people eat down here?" I asked the director, Ellen Baxter.

"No," she replied. "Some eat in their rooms or in the lounges, since each floor is equipped with kitchen facilities. Some like to eat together in this communal dining area, and some of the people who are less able to cope regularly eat downstairs. The way it works is simple." She added, "Our cooks, who are tenants, advertise on the bulletin board that they are cooking on a certain night. Then people sign up

Above: a single room at
the Heights, a model SRO.
Below: one of the
dining/recreation
rooms at the Heights.

for dinner, so the cook knows how many people to expect. Each person contributes two dollars towards the food, and sometimes people bring extras for everyone."

Each person has a private room. Bathrooms, with showers as well as bathtubs, and kitchenettes are located in the hallways for all tenants of that floor. The rooms are nice and cheery and big enough for a minimal amount of furniture.

"Do you realize that the Heights is the first new SRO built in the city since the 1970s?" Ellen said. While New York City demolished over one hundred thousand single-room units, where so many of these people once lived, it has not built any facilities to replace those units.

"Why didn't they build new places like the Heights?" I asked.

She replied that it was simply not economically advantageous for the landlords to build SROs, when they could instead convert them into units that sell for hundreds of thousands of dollars.

The Heights is a story of perseverance. Ellen Baxter and Kim Hopper had been working with the homeless long before most people realized that the homeless were not just a few "crazies" living on the streets because they like it that way. They began to do a major study in 1980,[28] getting facts about the homeless, estimating the actual numbers of the population, finding out who they were, why they were on the streets, and how they got into this situation.

She said that after years of working with the homeless population, she became very discouraged by the lack of progress. "After all the studies and all the attention, I

Director Ellen Baxter interviews an applicant for residency at the Heights.

– 80

found that the same people I saw years ago were still on the streets." She became more and more convinced that the problem of the homeless is the lack of housing—no available places to live. So she embarked on a project that took two years to launch—the Heights, a model for housing the homeless.

What it took to make the Heights a reality is a story of the triumph of will over bureaucracy, callousness, and endless red tape. This building was once like thousands of other buildings in poor areas. Most of them are still vacant for a number of reasons—the landlord either didn't pay the taxes or abandoned the building because it needed massive renovations, or there was a fire and the landlord refused or was unable to make repairs. Whatever the reason, many buildings are uninhabitable and empty, and as the years go by without needed repairs being made, they continue to deteriorate. The Heights building was empty for many years until the group now directing this operation decided to purchase the building from the city and renovate and convert it into single rooms for homeless people. After a two-year struggle to obtain a low-interest bank loan, to get investors interested in the renovation of the building, and to meet the dozens of regulations of the city building code—made more complicated because they often contradicted regulations specified by the state—the Heights opened its door to fifty-five people, one of whom not so long ago was described as follows:

> *Mary* was found on the far end of a Manhattan subway platform amid piles of newspapers and garbage. The odor emanating from her was literally nauseating. The first few times she was approached by an outreach worker, she refused contact and offers of food and coffee. Later she*

*The names and identifying information of all individuals mentioned here have been changed to assure anonymity.

accepted food and spoke of pain in her legs and removed the debris that surrounded her lower body. Upon seeing the condition of Mary's legs, the worker arranged for a nurse to bring buckets of water and cleaning solution onto the subway platform. Up to this time, Mary had refused to go to the emergency room of a nearby hospital because she had tried before and had been turned away. The nurse and social worker, fearing that Mary had gangrene, were eventually able to persuade Mary to try the hospital again. With the worker negotiating on her behalf, Mary was admitted and given intensive antibiotic treatments. Physicians involved with the case had previously known her illness to be [one] contracted [only] in the Third World. Surgery was performed and further improved her mobility. Following a two-month stay by Mary, the worker was notified that Mary would be discharged back to the streets. Mary was then placed by the worker in temporary accommodations until her move into the Heights.

Today, no one would recognize Mary based on that description. Mary is a testament to what it means to have a home—a warm, secure place to live. She is also proof that people living on the streets, on the edge of death, can be restored to the mainstream. The description of Mary as a homeless person reminded me of Fannie/Betty. Perhaps if Fannie were one of the fortunate living at the Heights instead of outside the ice-cream parlor, she might regain a respectable place in society.

It is hard to imagine that some of the people in this house are the same people who once huddled in doorways and were covered with filth, infested with lice, and sick. Today they participate in the management of this facility, sit on tenants' committees, and make their own rules and

*Residents of the Heights sitting
and talking in a small communal
living room located on the second
floor near their private rooms*

regulations, and treat their home with enormous respect. They won't let anyone destroy what took them so many years to build, a place called home.

Janice, a white woman in her late forties, was at the reception desk when I arrived. She asked if she could help me. I explained that I was expected by the director and some other residents. The director had suggested that I spend some time with Janice because she knew a lot about homelessness.

Janice began with a detailed explanation of the origin of homelessness in New York City, pointing to the demolition of SRO buildings, which created the housing shortage, and the nearly insurmountable problem of finding permanent apartments for low-income people. After an articulate and obviously thoughtful analysis on her part, I asked her why she was so interested in the problems of the homeless.

After a pause and a smile, she said, "I was homeless." She chuckled, knowing that I didn't expect that answer. "See how we stereotype everything? You didn't think I looked like I was homeless. There are plenty of people like me, once a real middle-class person who fell on hard times. It could happen to anybody. Maybe not the Rockefellers."

Yes, I had to admit she didn't look like a homeless person to me. She was educated, wore clean clothes, and worked the front desk in a highly professional way, directing traffic, giving people their phone messages, and introducing me to her neighbors, the other residents.

I wondered what had happened. How had she become homeless, living with people who were former mental patients, addicts, bums, and alcoholics?

Her story was a bit different from the rest, but then again, every homeless person has a different story.

Janice had had her own bookbinding business. She claims that her partner, responsible for the financial matters, failed in that job, and it became obvious that the business was in serious trouble. She needed money to salvage the business, and in order to do that, she decided to give up her apartment. She moved in with friends, but after a short while, there were terrible fights and she had to move again. But where? She had no money, and by this time her business was on the verge of collapse.

As she was trying to cope with this problem, she discovered she had cancer. While living on public assistance, she applied for disability insurance. Eventually she was placed in a facility for early retirement, a place that she claims was like an insane asylum. She had a room and a place to eat, but nothing more. She said that while she was there, she contemplated suicide many times. Then her luck turned, because a social worker she talked to had learned about the Heights and suggested that she be placed on their waiting list.

She was fortunate. After several months of waiting, she got in. She now lives there, still hoping to rebuild her business someday. She works at the front desk along with other residents, a job they are paid to do through a grant that the Heights received for job training. She spends the rest of her time talking to groups about being homeless, and she helps out at some of the shelters.

Janice was lucky that she never had to stay in shelters or on the streets. But after she gave up her home, she lost most of her belongings, and after her battle with cancer, she lost almost everything else.

Luis took over desk duty after Janice went upstairs to her room. Luis is an ex-alcoholic who came here from Santo Domingo. When he first came to New York at his sister's invitation, he was immediately confronted with a problem. His sister was a drug addict, a surprise to Luis. After a short stay with his sister, he tried to convince her to kick the habit. Instead of getting off drugs, however, one night when she was high, she threw Luis out of the house. He had no job, he didn't know anyone, and he had no money. Where could he go? For several months, Luis slept in one of the city shelters. Like most people who spend their nights in shelters, he spent his days wandering the streets and going to soup kitchens in search of his next meal. Luis tried to get a job, and he did manage to find a few odd jobs to make some money. But like other homeless people, he could not receive public assistance because he had no home address. But Luis was lucky, too. After less then a year of being homeless, he now has a home at the Heights.

He recalled the city shelter with terror. "The shelters are utilized by mostly black men. The whites, the Hispanics, and the older people are brutalized. The younger guys steal everything, they threaten people and intimidate everyone who can't defend themselves. As much as I could, I stayed to myself. It's hard to trust anyone. I tried to work sometimes during the day, but the money was barely enough for food. I could never have found an apartment with the money I occasionally earned. I am very grateful to this place. I was very fortunate."

Then there was Rebecca, who was not an ex-addict or an ex-alcoholic. She simply came home one night to see her building afire. After she spent a couple of nights on the street, a "nice lady" approached her and helped get her into a women's shelter. She stayed there for a few months, and when the Heights was ready for residents, she was offered a place. Today she works for the city of New York, helping to distribute clothing to shelters for the homeless.

Rebecca is very proud of her new home. For the Heights' first anniversary, she ordered a huge cake to celebrate. "I owe a lot to this place. It means a lot to me."

The stories at the Heights were not all happy ones, however. In the beginning, there were a lot of problems, as some of the ex-homeless had difficulty adjusting to a life without crime or to living with other people in the same house. The Heights has a tenants' committee. They help govern the building and handle any problems that may occur. Early on, they had a problem with crack, the highly addictive form of cocaine. Some of the tenants were using and selling crack on the premises, and instead of paying their rent as all tenants of the Heights were expected to do, they used the money to buy drugs. The other tenants were confronted with a very difficult and painful decision. What do you do with people living in your building who are not respecting the law and won't pay their rent? After some agonizing days and weeks, they decided that they had only one recourse. They had to begin the process of evicting some people.

"You have no idea how difficult it is for a person who had once been homeless to turn around and put a man on the streets," commented one resident. But in order to save their home, they knew that they had to do what was best for everyone.

It is not always easy for the homeless to adjust to a real home and an orderly life. Homelessness becomes a way of life. Some had forgotten how to live inside a house that is warm and how to spend the day working or looking for work. "I can't remember when I cooked last," commented a recent arrival at the Heights.

While I was talking to Janice and Luis, Rebecca came in from work. Some of the others, coming home from various activities, stopped by the desk to check messages, to socialize, and to chat about the one-year anniversary party. Mary, coming home from school, took the time to catch up on the gossip of the day. She is the baby of the house. She is only nineteen and stunningly beautiful. She had been homeless since she left the Caribbean area at thirteen. She had stayed in a variety of places, including group homes and shelters for runaways or other homeless youngsters. Now she goes to college, and, through government aid, she manages to pay rent while working part-time.

As everyone came in for the night, I thought about this extraordinary situation. Not so long ago, many of these people were on the streets or staying in shelters. Instead of living productive lives, they spent their days searching for food and shelter. Now, less than a year later, many of them are working, some are in school, and those in need of special assistance are getting the help they deserve.

Nevertheless, those years on the streets took their toll on many of these people. Most of them were not on the streets for a great length of time, some not at all. They were homeless, but they were in shelters or youth homes or other temporary facilities. However, some *had* lived on the streets for several years, riding subways and eating from garbage cans or handouts or soup kitchens. Today, because of the Heights, even those with a history of mental illness can live in dignity.

As people were busy coming and going out of the desk area, a young woman I had just interviewed came downstairs, very upset. She had locked herself out of her room, was panic-stricken, and wanted to call the director. Luis, the person on duty, gave her money to call from a phone booth outside. The phone at the desk is locked, and outgoing phone calls are not allowed. I found it ironic that a formerly homeless person would lock herself out.

Rebecca, who always had something to say, chuckled. "Are you kidding? People lock themselves out all the time. However, they usually give someone in the building an extra set of keys so that they can get back into their room."

But it made sense. For some of the people living at the Heights, having keys and responsibilities is a new or recently renewed experience. Besides, people who have lived in shelters or on the streets are not prone to trust others, so they don't think of giving anyone another set of their keys. It probably takes a while to get into the habit of locking doors again and to know how to have possessions again and trust neighbors again. And it must take years not to hear voices in the night.

"It took me months to sleep at night," said one formerly homeless resident. The homeless often sleep during the day because it is safer and stay up at night so they won't be robbed, mugged, or raped.

"Mugged or robbed? What do they take from you?" I asked, out of my belief that they had nothing left that anyone would want to take from them.

One of the residents responded, smiling, "They'll take your leftover sandwich, steal your shoes, your blanket. Somehow other homeless people have even less then you."

There are plans to develop another facility, modeled on the Heights, this time for families. Of course, it will take a year or two before it opens, and the new facility will house less than 100 people.

The Heights is one permanent solution to an ever-growing problem—the shortage of housing for poor and low-income people. Some will say that it is like a drop of water in the sea. Indeed it is. The Heights can accommodate only fifty-five people. Obviously, this cannot have a major impact on the hundreds of thousands who are homeless. Nonetheless, it is a model for what can be accomplished with determination and willingness to find an alternative to the streets and temporary shelter. It also testifies to the ability of the human spirit to rejuvenate itself and flourish again.

As many advocates for the homeless argue, if only the federal and city governments would cooperate with these ventures to renovate old, dilapidated buildings instead of pouring money into the pockets of landlords who own the filthy, barely habitable welfare hotels—which often cost more than luxury apartments—perhaps together all of us can find a solution to this ever-growing human tragedy.

7
WHAT HAS CHANGED?
WHERE DO WE
GO FROM HERE?

From 1980 to 1987, the homeless population soared to an astonishing number that is still increasing every year. For example, New York City in 1987 sheltered more than 4,600 families, a 13 percent increase from 1985. New Jersey has a homeless population of 26,000; Connecticut, more than 12,000. Wherever we turn, we hear about the new homeless population. Even New York suburbs and areas such as Suffolk and Westchester counties report that their numbers of homeless people are in the several thousands.

But along with the rise in the number of homeless and the change in the composition of the homeless population, there is also a change in the public's attitude and awareness that has come from watching the homeless become a regular and permanent fixture among us. The Heights is just one example of that change.

The Heights is an exceptional model for community housing, but there are many others. Hundreds of organizations have emerged (including Women in Need, the National Coalition for the Homeless, the First Moravian Church, the Bethlehem Haven) to help the homeless. Throughout the country, numerous groups are working to find solutions to this problem. City governments are begin-

A demonstration at New York's
City Hall in the spring of 1987
in support of housing for the homeless

ning to realize that they can't ignore the homeless or simply pass ordinances against them.

Santa Barbara, California, a city of affluence, is a case in point. In 1979 the city reacted to an influx of homeless people by passing an ordinance banning sleeping and camping in public places. That ordinance was followed by others outlawing drinking in public and banning the homeless from voting in elections. From 1984 to 1986, at least 1,000 homeless people were arrested for sleeping in city parks, on the streets, and on the beaches. During this time, too, two homeless men were killed.[29] At an Easter service for the homeless in 1986, the Reverend Alan McCoy asked God to forgive the city fathers for engaging in what was described as a systematic program to arrest and prosecute the homeless merely for sleeping in public places.

Mitch Snyder—director of the Community for Creative Nonviolence, based in Washington, D.C., a national advocacy organization for the homeless—threatened to inundate Santa Barbara with thousands of homeless people if the city did not change what he called its "ignorant and selfish ways." At a news conference, he said: "We are sick and tired of watching and reading and hearing of the vulgarity of the treatment of the homeless in Santa Barbara."

A few months later, the mayor and the City Council, facing a nationally orchestrated demonstration by Mitch Snyder and the Community for Creative Nonviolence to overturn a ban against sleeping in public, voted to repeal the ordinance. In addition to the repeal of this ordinance, virtually all of Santa Barbara's ordinances that would affect the homeless have been challenged and overturned in court, including the one that prevents the homeless from voting.

The Coalition for the Homeless and its president, Robert Hayes, are still waging and winning battles throughout the country to improve the status of the homeless. In March 1987, the New York State Supreme Court's Appellate Term found that a state law that bars loitering in transit centers is unconstitutional because it does not define

Robert Hayes, president of the National Coalition for the Homeless, and homeless youngster David Bright, ten years old, testified in 1986 before the Congressional Select Committee on Hunger.

which acts it prohibits and because such centers are public spaces.

"What it means is that homeless people can't be arrested simply on the basis of their status," said a lawyer for the Legal Aid Society, which brought the appeal. According to the Coalition for the Homeless, about 1,500 homeless people stay in New York City's midtown terminals every night, and countless others at Penn Station and in subway tunnels, lying in rows, sleeping on newspapers and cardboard boxes. The court's decision was a small victory, for as Robert Hayes said "[It gives them] the right to stay in a terrible place."

Between 1982 and 1984, the infant mortality rate in New York City's welfare hotels had surpassed the rates of the city's poorest neighborhoods and even those of some of the world's developing nations. For every 1,000 births to homeless women housed in hotels by the city, the New York City Health Department recorded twenty-five infant deaths under the age of one.[30]

One organization working to reduce such grim statistics is Women in Need, started by Rita Zimmer. Several years ago she convinced the elders of the Church of Saint Mary the Virgin in New York to allow her to use their empty mission house as a shelter for homeless women. The shelter would provide a "dignified, safe and more compassionate" alternative to the crowded welfare hotels. In 1983 the shelter opened. In its first year, Women in Need survived on a $20,000 federal grant as well as what Rita Zimmer contributed from her own savings. By 1986, Women in Need was feeding eight mothers and nine children living in the shelter. In addition, the shelter fed nearly 100 destitute women and children daily who were living in hotels without cooking facilities.

In three years Women in Need grew from an idea supported by $50 donations into a program with an annual budget of $650,000 and a full-time staff of twenty: social workers, counselors, and a housing specialist, who help homeless families find decent housing.

Women in Need has facilities operating in other sections of New York, as well, such as Casa Rita in the Bronx, which cost $500,000 to renovate and refurbish. This former Roman Catholic school is now a spotless white brick building with an awning over the entranceway, and it looks like a comfortable home where women and children can live in dignity. Future plans include two more shelters, a day-care center for working mothers, and a day camp for eighty children.

These shelters operated by Women in Need can accommodate only a small percentage of those in need. But they are a major step in the right direction because they provide a decent place to stay and offer assistance with permanent housing. There are also special shelters for men who are working. Men with jobs but without homes have difficulty staying at the city shelters because at the end of the day they can't get back to the shelters in time to secure a bed. (Homeless men usually begin lining up in the late afternoon to make sure they have a place to sleep.) Added to that problem, they also have difficulty getting a good night's rest because of the noise that is a constant annoyance in those shelters. Some have found a solution to the problem in the opening of a new shelter for working men in Brooklyn, New York, where 100 men live.

To get into the program, the men must sign a contract agreeing to put half their salaries into a savings account and attend workshops on personal hygiene, how to look for an apartment, how to budget their money, and in general, how to take responsibility for their lives. According to the program director, since its inception, forty-five men have moved out, half of whom now have known addresses. Some were sent to other shelters because they refused to follow the rules, while several others lost their jobs and were required to leave.

The shelter is far from luxurious, but it is certainly a

great improvement over the city shelters. But again, what are 100 men among the tens of thousands who are homeless in New York City? For the few, this shelter provides the help they need to put them on their feet.

The Manhattan Bowery Corporation is also a major service provider for the homeless. In July 1986, they announced plans to open a fifty-bed home for mentally ill men and women now living on the streets—a residence that will offer sorely needed supervised long-term care. Programs like the Manhattan Bowery project are crucial for the mentally ill homeless population, since three-quarters of them reject shelters because they have been abused and are afraid of these huge places. Supervised residential care, in a warm and professional environment, is the only solution to the mentally ill homeless crisis.

Saint Francis, another program that houses the mentally ill homeless, has 300 rooms in three buildings and provides another alternative to the streets and doorways of Grand Central Station. Saint Francis houses and treats people for $20 a day as opposed to $150 a day at a state institution or $500 at Bellevue Hospital—at taxpayers' expense. Again though, Saint Francis reaches a mere fraction of the people who need help.

Along with Project Help, which allows city officials and police officers to bring social workers, physicians, and nurses to the assistance of street dwellers, there are several programs to help the mentally ill homeless, who at times refuse to go into shelters even when the temperature is below freezing. While the police are empowered to force them to go into shelters if the temperature falls below freezing, one program follows up the enforcement by providing care and services, including medical help. Although professional care for the homeless is inadequate, there is recognition that different programs are needed to provide the care that the extremely diverse homeless population so desperately needs. In 1986, a few days before Christmas, on the first day of winter and the darkest day of the year,

in a symbolic gesture, more than 1,000 people in Manhattan marched through the city in a candlelight vigil for the city's homeless and hungry. As Paul Gorman, one of the organizers, put it, "I think you're seeing the seeds of a housing justice movement that's going to be like the civil rights movement."[31] The coalition collected 20,000 pounds of food for the homeless at 40 sites, and 300 volunteers spruced up buildings in Harlem and on the Lower East Side. They also collected over 4,000 signatures on a petition asking the city to provide permanent housing in vacant buildings owned by the city for families with annual incomes of less than $25,000. While volunteers and good-intentioned people cannot solve the homeless crisis, they have created a climate that has forced the government to take action on behalf of the homeless.

By 1987, members of Congress, film stars, and investment bankers had spent a night on the cold streets of Washington to dramatize the problem. Representative Mickey Leland, a Democrat from Texas, remarked, "It's amazing, there's really a dramatic difference between the heat grates and the ground." Congressman Leland and 100 others had spent a night of below-freezing temperatures on a Capitol Hill street corner to demonstrate their concern for the nation's homeless and rally support for a $500 million emergency-aid bill to help them.

Martin Sheen, the actor, also took part in the demonstration and slept on the bare ground wrapped in a blanket.

*A few days before Christmas
in 1986 in New York City,
over a thousand people took
part in a candlelight vigil
for the homeless and hungry.
Among the demonstrators was
four-year-old Kenya Ellison,
one of the homeless.*

– 99

He observed, "The stories are familiar ones we've been hearing for years. They always start with one stroke of bad luck which leads to despair and disintegration."[32]

Chicago's mayor, Harold Washington, also joined the group sleeping on the streets. He said, "We weren't trying to [re-] create the trauma of a homeless, powerless person who is out there night after night. We were trying to indicate through this act that we sympathize with them. We are saying we recognize you, we know you exist, and we are trying to do something to help you."[33]

On March 5, 1987, the *New York Times* reported, "The House of Representatives today approved a bill of new aid for the homeless that could cost $725 million." Though only a step forward and not a permanent solution, this action demonstrates that at last some powerful politicians have heard the public outcry. Now that well-known public figures are taking part in demonstrations and pushing for necessary funds, some aid is finally being provided.

The problem is huge, and there are no simple, overnight solutions. It stems from the numerous changes that have occurred in contemporary American society, including changes in family structure, the great increase in the number of single mothers—especially among teenagers, high unemployment among certain groups, the deinstitutionalization of mental patients, and the dramatic housing crisis.

We have come a long way from the time when people thought that the homeless were a handful of crazies and drunks who could not fit into civilized society. Now more people recognize that homelessness is a major problem facing millions of people and that the government must find the funds to help eradicate it, that small, humanitarian groups alone cannot provide the solution. According to a Roper poll for the *Atlanta Journal and Constitution*, taking care of the homeless was a major concern among 73 percent of the Democrats and 55 percent of the Republicans in the South. In comparison, abortion ranked about 50 percent and Star Wars at 33 percent as issues of serious concern.

"We reaffirm the principle that decent shelter and affordable housing are fundamental rights in a civilized society," says Robert Hayes, of the Coalition for the Homeless. As a civilized society, we are beginning to show that we care. It is not enough to pass legislation adding $725 million to aid for the homeless, but at least we are demonstrating that we are a society that will try to solve this problem. We are recognizing that the problem will not go away if we lock people up for sleeping in parks and on sidewalks. Some have had the courage and the compassion to begin to become involved in a struggle that is a long way from being won. They will not stand by and watch or step over the homeless. They have said yes to our recognition that we care, to our awareness that we could ourselves become homeless and that we cannot just look the other way and let this injustice go on.

It has already gone on too long. Too many people have suffered and far too many have died unnecessarily because no one cared or for the lack of money. It should never have happened in the twentieth century, in the wealthiest country in the world. We can only hope that the tide has turned and that no one else will die for the lack of a home.

SOURCE NOTES

INTRODUCTION

1. "The Homeless Become an Issue," *New York Times,* February 7, 1987, p. A8.
2. Conversation with Ellen Baxter, Board of Directors, Coalition for the Homeless.
3. Suzanne Daley, "Record Number of People Appear at New York City's Crowded Emergency Shelters," *New York Times,* January 27, 1987, p. B2.
4. "The Homeless," *Newsweek,* November, 1986, p. 12.
5. Statistics from New York City Human Resources Administration, 1984 survey.
6. Ibid.
7. "Homeless Families to Double This Year, A Report Predicts," *New York Times,* January 12, 1980, p. A4.

CHAPTER ONE

8. Robert M. Hayes, "The Issue Is Housing," *New York Times,* November 17, 1986, p. B5.
9. "Abandoned," *Newsweek,* January 6, 1986, p. 14.
10. Crystal Nix, "Housing Family in a Shelter Costs City $70,000 a Year," *New York Times,* March 7, 1986, p. B3.

CHAPTER TWO

11. *Homeless in Phoenix: Testimony before House Sub-committee on Housing and Community Development* (New York: National Coalition for the Homeless, May 1984).
12. Ibid., p. 14.
13. Ibid., p. 23.
14. Ibid., p. 8.
15. Ibid., p. 8.
16. "Out in the Cold," *Arizona Republic*, December 18, 1983, p. 25.
17. *Mid-America in Crisis: Homeless in Des Moines* (New York: National Coalition for the Homeless, 1986), p. 29.
18. Ibid., p. 21.
19. Ibid., p. 23.
20. Ibid., p. 30.
21. Ibid., p. 4.
22. Ibid., p. 17.
23. Ibid., p.19.
24. Ibid., p. 2.
25. "A Psychiatrist to the Poor Tells the Toll of Uprooted Life on Families and the Friendless," *People*, February 10, 1986, p. 86.

CHAPTER FIVE

26. Barbara Basler, "City's Homeless: Portrait of a Growing and Varied Population," *New York Times*, November 17, 1986, p. B5.
27. "The New Homeless Has Its Roots in Economics," *New York Times*, March 16, 1986, p. D5.

CHAPTER SIX

28. Ellen Baxter and Kim Hooper, *Private Lives/Public Spaces: Homeless Adults on the Streets of New York City* (New York: Community Service Society, 1981).

CHAPTER SEVEN

29. Marcia Chambers, "Santa Barbara Moves Against the Homeless Draw Protests," *New York Times*, March 31, 1986, p. 8.
30. Barbara Basler, "Infant Death Rate Is High in Welfare Hotels," *New York Times*, June 10, 1986, p. B3.
31. Conversation with Paul Gorman, December 1986.
32. "Chilly Night on a Sidewalk Grate Teaches Lesson about Homeless," *New York Times*, March 5, 1987, p. A25.
33. Ibid.

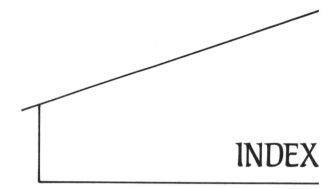

INDEX

Homeless children
(continued)
   in New York (city), 70
   number of, 12
   and pregnancy, 27
   program for, 72, 74
   and school, 70, 71, 74
     75
Homeless families
   case examples of, 71
   living conditions of,
     67–68, 71
   in New York, 67–68
   number of, 12, 67
Homelessness
   causes of, 12, 17–24,
     33, 100
   definition of, 72, 75
   and deinstitutionaliza-
     tion, 18–22
   and demolition of
     single room
     occupancy (SRO)
     hotels, 17–18
   and government
     policies, 12, 18–21,
     22–24, 90, 99
   and mental illness, 13,
     18–21
   requested legislation
     on, 99, 100
   rising rates of, 27
   Roper poll on, 100
   and scarcity of low-
     income housing, 22
   See also Iowa,
     homelessness in

Hooper, Kim, 80
Housing
   abandoned buildings
     as, 90
   in Arizona, 30
   cost of, 24, 68
   and federal housing
     assistance, 68
   low-income, 22, 68
   scarcity of, 22
   and the Reagan
     administration, 68
   shortage of, 90
Human Resources Admin-
   istration (New York
   City), 27

Incomes, low, 18, 22
Iowa
   evictions in, 37
   farm crisis in, 35–37
   homelessness in, 34–38
   poverty rate in, 35–37
   See also Shelters

Manhattan Bowery
   Corporation, 97
Mental illness
   in Arizona, 30
   Community Mental
     Health Centers Act,
     21
   as cause of
     homelessness, 13,
     18–21
   and deinstitutionaliza-
     tion, 18–22